JUL   1994

J
796.334
Bar   Barrett, Norman S.

The World Cup

DUE DATE			
4/98-11			
			21223

THE WORLD CUP

Norman Barrett

Thomson Learning
New York

Cover picture Scifo of Belgium (left) tussles with Spain's
Roberto in the 1990 World Cup tournament.
Title page Argentina's Mario Kempes on the ball in the 1978
World Cup final against the Netherlands.

Photographs supplied by Colorsport, Syndication
International, Norman Barrett, Allsport, Bob Thomas Sports
Photography, United Press International
Diagram by Drawing Attention

Published in the United States by
Thomson Learning
115 Fifth Avenue
New York, NY 10003

Published simultaneously in Great Britain by
Wayland (Publishers) Ltd.

Library of Congress Cataloging-in-Publication Data
Barrett, Norman S.
  The World Cup / Norman Barrett.
       p.   cm.
  Includes bibliographical references and index.
  ISBN 1-56847-124-6 : $15.95
  1. World Cup (Soccer) — Juvenile literature. 2. Soccer —
Juvenile literature. I. Title.
GV943.25.B37   1993
796.334'668 — dc20   93-21660

Printed in Italy

Contents

Introduction

Soccer's World Cup is a great festival of soccer that puts the world's leading players on show in an exciting tournament to find the world's best.

*T*he World Cup ranks with the Olympic Games as one of the greatest competitions of world sports. Twenty-four of the best soccer-playing nations from all continents come together every four years for the finals tournament of the World Cup.

Only the country that is chosen to host the finals tournament and the winners of the previous World Cup are sure of their places. The others have to qualify by playing each other in groups. These start nearly two years before the finals tournament.

▷ **Opposite page: England captain Bobby Moore – hoisted on teammates' shoulders – holds the Jules Rimet Trophy in 1966.**

▽ **Action from the first World Cup final, which took place in Montevideo, Uruguay, in 1930. Argentina's goalkeeper dives in vain as the host country Uruguay scores the third goal of their 4-2 victory.**

The World Cup is organized by the governing body of soccer (or football, as it is called in Europe), the Fédération Internationale de Football Association (FIFA). FIFA was founded in 1904, but it was another 26 years before the first World Cup tournament took place.

There were just 13 nations in Uruguay to contest the first World Cup. It has grown enormously since then, and teams representing more than 140 countries take part in the qualifying stages.

The original trophy was named after Jules Rimet, a Frenchman who was president of FIFA from 1920 to 1954.

The current trophy is the FIFA World Cup, presented after Brazil won the Jules Rimet Trophy for the third time in 1970.

World Cup facts

✔ Only six countries have won the World Cup – Brazil, Italy, and Germany (three times each), Uruguay and Argentina (twice), and England (once).
✔ Five of the 14 World Cup tournaments have been won by the host country.
✔ Italy and Mexico are the only countries to have hosted two World Cups.

Staging the Cup

A month-long feast of soccer, with more than 50 matches, reaches a climax when the last two countries left battle it out in the World Cup final.

In the qualifying competition, teams play in six continental zones: Europe, South America, Africa, Asia, Oceania (Australia, New Zealand, and some Pacific islands), and a zone made up of North and Central America and the Caribbean region. Each zone stages its own competitions, and the successful countries go to the finals tournament.

The number of teams from each continent in the finals tournament depends on the soccer-playing strength of its countries. There are places in the tournament for 12 or 13 teams from Europe, with another 3 or 4 places allocated to South America, the other stronghold of soccer. The remaining places are divided among the other continents, although the winner of the Oceania zone usually has to play off against a country from another continent.

In the finals tournament itself, the 24 teams are divided into six groups of four. The teams in a group play each other once, and the top two teams in each group and the best four of the rest go through to the last sixteen. From then it becomes a single-elimination tournament.

Before the final, the two losing semifinalists play each other in a match to decide third place.

◁ *David O'Leary scores the deciding goal for the Republic of Ireland in the penalty "shoot-out" with Romania in the last 16 of the 1990 World Cup.*

The field of play

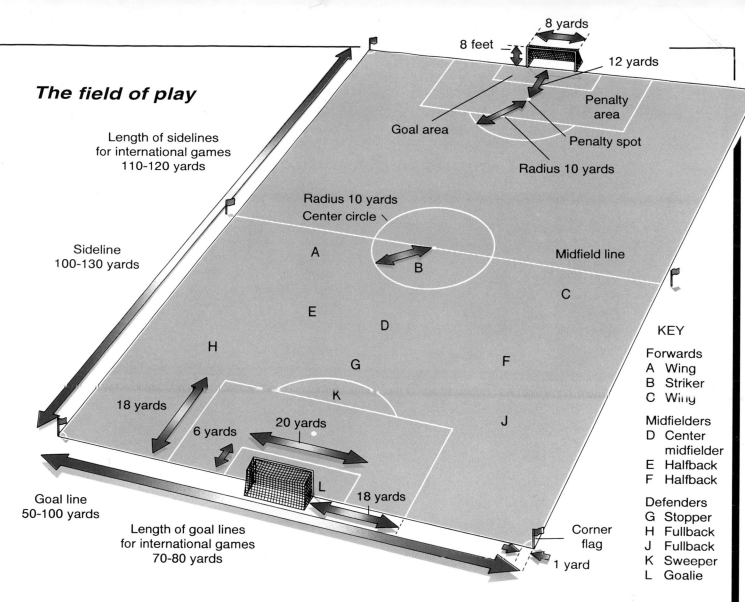

8 yards

8 feet

12 yards

Goal area

Penalty area

Penalty spot

Radius 10 yards

Length of sidelines
for international games
110-120 yards

Radius 10 yards
Center circle

Midfield line

Sideline
100-130 yards

A

B

C

E

D

H

G

F

K

J

18 yards

6 yards

20 yards

L

18 yards

Goal line
50-100 yards

Length of goal lines
for international games
70-80 yards

Corner
flag

1 yard

KEY

Forwards
A Wing
B Striker
C Wing

Midfielders
D Center
   midfielder
E Halfback
F Halfback

Defenders
G Stopper
H Fullback
J Fullback
K Sweeper
L Goalie

△ *The official dimensions of a soccer field are stated in yards. These rules allow considerable variations in size.*

The shoot-out

In the single-elimination stages of the World Cup finals, there is no time for rematches. So if two teams are tied after the regular 90 minutes of play, two overtime periods of 15 minutes each way are played. If the teams are still tied, the result is decided on a penalty "shoot-out."

Five players from each team are selected to take penalty kicks. The teams alternate penalty kicks. Each player is allowed a single attempt from the penalty spot. If the shot is stopped, the player does not get another

chance to score. The team with more goals out of five attempts wins. If the score is still tied, the shoot out continues with the remaining players until a winner emerges.

FIFA is experimenting with a "sudden-death" method in the junior league. This means that the first team to score in overtime would win. Only if there were no goals after the 30 minutes of overtime would a shoot-out take place. If this works well in the junior league, the rule will be introduced in the 1998 World Cup.

World Cup heroes

The World Cup is remembered for great players such as Pelé, Cruyff, and Maradona. But there have also been some unlikely heroes who have starred on the World Cup stage.

For one month every four years, the World Cup is the focus of soccer players and fans. Every goal, every save, every incident in the 52 matches is shown on television, replayed in slow motion, and discussed by experts. Players, officials, and coaches are praised and criticized by spectators, by commentators, and by millions of armchair viewers in their own homes. But when all the arguments are finished, it is the star performers who are remembered most – the popular heroes of the World Cup.

Not all World Cup heroes are goal-scorers. Everyone has a part to play in soccer, and some of the most memorable performances have come from goalkeepers and defenders.

△ *The great Pelé shields the ball with his leg and body as he tries to dribble past his marker Alan Mullery in the Brazil-England game in 1970.*

◁ *England striker Geoff Hurst scores his third goal to round off England's 4-2 victory over Germany in the 1966 World Cup final. Hurst had been regarded by many fans as no more than a hard worker. But he became a World Cup hero, the only player to score a hat trick in a final.*

△ *Johan Cruyff (orange shirt) is brought down when going for goal in the first minute of the 1974 World Cup final. A penalty was given and the Dutch took the lead, but Germany went on to win 2-1.*

Superstar Cruyff

The Dutch captain Johan Cruyff was the star of the 1974 World Cup. Cruyff led the Netherlands to the final with an exciting brand of soccer that thrilled the crowds and defeated Brazil and Argentina on the way.

In the final, he produced a sparkling run from his own half in the very first minute that took him through the German defense and into their penalty area before he was tripped. The Netherlands scored from the penalty that followed but lost the game.

Among the truly great players who have shone on the World Cup stage are Pelé of Brazil, the Dutch star Johan Cruyff, and the Argentinian "wizard" Diego Maradona. These were players who could dominate a game and delight the fans with dazzling shows of skill.

Gordon Banks of England took fans' breath away with some of his saves. The German sweeper Franz Beckenbauer controlled the game from the back. And the veteran Cameroon striker Roger Milla inspired his unfavored team to reach the quarterfinals in 1990.

Goalkeepers

The players who tend goal are among the bravest in soccer, hurling themselves to and fro in their efforts to block shots or to pluck the ball from the heads and feet of opposing players.

Good goalkeeping calls for a variety of skills as well as courage and fine judgment. A goalie needs sure hands to catch the ball cleanly or to knock it to safety. Goalies need to be fairly tall and very agile in order to cover all corners of the goal. Speed is also important for racing out to beat an opponent to the ball or to smother a shot.

A goalkeeper must be master of the penalty area, making important decisions whether to come out or to stay between the posts, calling out instructions to fellow defenders, and ready to start the offense with an accurate throw or kick.

The goalie is the last line of defense, so any mistakes are usually costly ones.

▽ *Gordon Banks won a World Cup winner's medal with England in 1966, but he is remembered most for his save against Pelé in the game versus Brazil in 1970. Banks looked stranded when Pelé's downward header hit the ground (bottom left picture), but somehow he managed to dive full length and scoop the ball up to safety (right).*

Although goalkeepers are regarded as "crazy" by fellow soccer players because of the risks they take, they generally enjoy longer careers than most other players. Dino Zoff was 40 years old when he captained Italy to their World Cup success in 1982. Pat Jennings made his last appearance for Northern Ireland on his 41st birthday, against Brazil in the 1986 World Cup. And England's Peter Shilton was nearly 41 when he played his last game for England in the 1990 World Cup.

Goalkeeping facts and feats

✔ *Mexican goalie Antonio Carbajal is the only player to have appeared in five World Cup tournaments (1950-66).*
✔ *Among the goalies who hold their country's record for most international appearances are England's Peter Shilton with 125 caps (a world record), Northern Ireland's Pat Jennings (119), and Italy's Dino Zoff (112).*
✔ *Most successful teams have reliable goalkeepers. But Brazil won the 1970 Cup despite the blunders of their erratic goalie, Félix.*

Defenders

The true soccer fan appreciates good defense, and some excellent fullbacks and central defenders have earned their place in World Cup history alongside their more spectacular teammates.

*T*he first concern of defenders is to disrupt their opponents' offensive moves. They do this by getting to the ball before their opponents by tackling an opponent who has the ball or by making it difficult for an opponent to pass or shoot.

But defenders must be able to make good use of the ball when they win it, to start up their own offense. And they play their part in offense. The fullbacks make runs along the wings and cross the ball into the center. The tall central defenders move up into the opposition goalmouth for corners and free kicks, where their heading power is an important offensive weapon.

Man of vision

England captain in the 1966 and 1970 World Cups, Bobby Moore was one of those rare players who had a complete picture of the pattern of play in his mind at all times. He could settle the ball, turn, and, without looking up, hit an accurate pass to a teammate 30 or 40 yards away.

He developed this knack as a young player. Throughout a game he would ask himself: "If I got the ball now, how would I use it?"

◁ England fullback Stuart Pearce not only has a fierce tackle, but he can cross the ball like a wing and possesses a rocketlike shot. Here he is shown hitting one of his deadly free kicks for Nottingham Forest.

There are two main methods of defending. In zone defense, which employs a "back four" of two fullbacks and two central defenders, each defender takes on any opponent who moves into a certain area of the field. Brazil and most British teams employ a zone defense. It calls for a good understanding among the defenders and considerable practice.

Most other countries use a sweeper and man-for-man marking. In this method, each defender has a particular opponent to mark, except for a player at the back, the sweeper, who is free to move across the field. The sweeper covers his fellow defenders and picks up any balls played through or over the defense. Defenders must be able to play anywhere – left, right, or center – because they may have to follow the player they are marking to any part of the field. Sweepers need to be able to spot danger and cover it.

Defenders – facts and feats

✔ Uruguayan defender José Batista earned the dubious distinction of the quickest ever ejection in a World Cup match. He was given a red card after just 50 seconds of the game against Scotland in Mexico in 1986.

✔ Central defender Luisito Monti played in two World Cup finals for different countries. He was on the losing side in 1930 with Argentina, but earned a winner's medal for Italy in 1934.

✔ Italy's fullback Antonio Cabrini became the first – and so far the only – player to miss a penalty kick in a World Cup final when his shot went wide against Germany in 1982.

✔ The winning goal in the 1990 final was scored from the penalty spot by Germany's Andreas Brehme.

◁ *Italy's fullback Paolo Maldini (right) tackles an Austrian player in the 1990 World Cup. Maldini, who plays for AC Milan, is one of the world's most skillful defenders.*

Midfielders 1

Midfield is like a busy traffic corner. The players who operate there control the game, setting up offense and disrupting the opposition.

*T*he midfield general, or playmaker, must be a good tactician because he is responsible for directing his team's offense. He should always be available for passes from defenders, linking defense with offense.

This role also calls for excellent control in order to hold the ball long enough to create an opening. When the playmaker sees or creates an opportunity, he must also have the ability to split the opposing defense with an accurate pass.

△*England's Bobby Charlton (right) in action in the 1970 World Cup.*

Goals from midfield

Bobby Charlton, of Manchester United and England, was originally a striker and then a wing. He became a midfield general in the mid-1960s. He had the ability to spray long passes to all parts of the field, with the extra menace of a powerful shot with either foot. He retired from international soccer in 1970 with 106 caps, and his record of 49 goals for England has not been equaled.

◁ *French star Michel Platini (in blue), like Charlton, possessed a deadly shot.*

△ *Argentina's Diego Maradona chips the ball over an Italian opponent in the 1986 World Cup.*

In modern top-class soccer, many coaches feel that a team should not be too dependent on one player, which means there are fewer midfield generals than there used to be. The truly great ones, such as Holland's Ruud Gullit and Frank Rijkaard and England's Paul Gascoigne, have the ability to change the course of a game with one flash of genius, and they are exciting players to watch.

There should always be a place in the game for players with imagination. Many teams pack the midfield with ball-winners and runners, but most fans would like to see a playmaker using his skills and his brain.

Maradona – his two sides

Although small, Diego Maradona is exceptionally strong. His masterly ball control enabled him to jink and squeeze through the tightest of defenses. He played in Argentina's First Division at the age of 15 and for his country at 16.

He directs his team's play, moving upfield with a series of short passes. Then he may make a defense-splitting pass or go for goal himself. He has inspired every team he played for, and in 1986 he led Argentina to World Cup victory.

Sadly, there was a darker side to Maradona. He was ejected in the 1982 World Cup for a bad foul against Brazil. Against England in the 1986 World Cup, he scored with a deliberate handball, unseen by the referee. And he was banned from soccer in 1991 for 15 months for taking drugs.

Midfielders 2

◁ **Dynamic Dutch midfielder Johan Neeskens in action against Argentina in the 1978 World Cup.**

The midfielder whose main task is to prevent the opponents from gaining momentum is known as the anchorman. He is also called a "spoiler" or "marker."

The anchorman is usually also the midfield ball-winner. But this is not always just a defensive job, and players such as former England captain Bryan Robson have scored many goals by acting as offensive midfielders, too.

The "toothless terror"

△ **Nobby Stiles (right) wins the ball with an overhead kick against France in 1966.**

The offensive midfielder's chief job is to sneak unnoticed through the opposing defense and get into goal-scoring positions. Such players are sometimes called midfield dynamos. They have lots of stamina and seem to be able to run for the whole 90 minutes, doing their share of defensive duties, too.

Johan Neeskens, Dutch World Cup star of the 1970s, and England's David Platt are fine examples of offensive midfielders. Such players inspire their teams with the force and energy of their game and score many key goals.

The role of anchorman originated in the 1960s, with teams struggling to dominate the midfield. England's victory in the 1966 World Cup owed much to their anchorman, Norbert "Nobby" Stiles of Manchester United.

Stiles was small, losing his hair, and missing some teeth. But he was a marvelous battler with a tigerish tackle that terrorized much bigger opponents.

Wings

Once, every team had two wings, providing some of soccer's most exciting moments as they raced along the sidelines and swung their crosses into the goalmouth. Where are they now?

Wings flourished in soccer until the 1966 World Cup. This was won by England's "wingless wonders," so called because manager Alf Ramsey played just two strikers up front, with backs and midfielders making runs on the wings. He used this strategy because he felt he did not have any wings good enough. It worked – and other teams began to play without wings, too.

◁ **Brazil's Garrincha (left) wards off the challenge of England's Ray Wilson in the 1962 World Cup. Garrincha overcame severe disability at birth to become the outstanding wing of the 1958 and 1962 World Cups.**

Strikers

A striker's chief job is to score goals. Strikers take up goal-scoring positions and shoot the ball on goal from all angles with head or foot at every opportunity.

Strikers play up front. They are the chief means of scoring. Some teams play only one striker. Others play two or even three.

Aside from taking shots on goal, strikers play their part in the development of offense. They take passes from their defenders or midfielders and hold the ball until teammates can join the offense and take a pass. Strikers whose chief job this is are called "target men."

▽ *England striker Gary Lineker slides in to score against Paraguay in the 1986 World Cup. Lineker scored most of his goals from close in. He had the gift of being in the right place at the right time, and his finishing was first class.*

Frank Klopas (in white) of the United States gets in an acrobatic shot on goal despite the attentions of his high-kicking opponent in a 1989 World Cup qualifying game against Trinidad and Tobago.

*T*arget men are usually tall and strong, so that they can withstand the challenges of big central defenders and compete for the ball in the air. They score their share of goals. But most of the great goal-scorers have been smaller men.

England's Gary Lineker and Germany's Gerd Müller are good examples of small goal-scoring strikers. Powerful thighs and a low center of gravity enabled them to turn and win loose balls in the goalmouth, popping them into the back of the net before their opponents realized the danger.

Teams with twin strikers up front but without wings expect their strikers to make runs to the wings. Since the new rule preventing goalkeepers from handling passes from teammates, strikers also have to make it hard for opposing goalies to clear the ball.

Striking facts and feats

✔ Paolo Rosi scored the most goals in the World Cup of 1982 – six – all of which were made in the last three games.
✔ German striker Gerd Müller scored the record total of 14 goals in two World Cups, 10 in 1970 and 4 in 1974.
✔ No player has scored five goals in a match in any finals tournament. The last player to score four was Spanish striker Emilio Butragueño, against Denmark in 1986.
✔ The only player to score in two successive World Cup finals was Brazilian striker Vavá, in 1958 against Sweden (two) and 1962 against Czechoslovakia.

French striker Just Fontaine scored 13 goals in the 1958 finals tournament, seven more than any other player that year.

Winners and losers

Although the lasting glory goes to the winning teams, some of the most memorable World Cup moments have been produced by the losers and their star performers.

For many countries, just reaching the finals tournament is a proud feat, and any victories bring great joy. But for the major soccer powers of Europe and South America, such as Germany and Brazil, only winning the World Cup is good enough. Defeat, even in the final, is regarded as failure.

Among the finest teams not to win the World Cup were Hungary, beaten finalists in 1954, and the Netherlands in 1974 and 1978. Portugal reached the semifinals in 1966, thanks largely to Eusebio, one of the World Cup greats. Denmark had a wonderful run in the 1986 World Cup, winning all three of its group matches before losing to Spain in the single-elimination stage.

A bad time to lose

△ *Hungary's captain Ferenc Puskas (left) in action in the 1954 World Cup final.*

Hungary dominated soccer in the early 1950s. The team lost only once in 51 internationals between 1950 and 1955 – and that was the final of the 1954 World Cup. Earlier the team had beaten Germany 8-3 in a group match, but lost to them 3-2 in the final.

◁ *Eusebio (far left) scores the first of his four goals against North Korea in 1966. Portugal was down 3-0 , but won 5-3.*

▷ *Scotland's Kenny Dalglish scores in 1978 against the Netherlands. Scotland won 3-2, but it was not enough for the team to progress. Scotland has qualified for the finals tournament eight times, but has never gotten past the first round.*

Supremos

Most countries put one man in charge of team selection and coaching – the team manager, coach, or supremo, as he is often called.

Two men have both played in and managed winning World Cup teams. Mário Zagalo was involved in all three of Brazil's successes – as a defender in 1958 and 1962, and as team manager in 1970. Franz Beckenbauer (pictured right) captained the winning German team in 1974 and was supremo in 1990.

Soccer hot spots

Europe and South America are the traditional strongholds of soccer, and no team from outside these continents has reached a World Cup final.

*E*urope is where soccer began, in Britain, and it is where most of the strongest soccer-playing nations are to be found. The continent's seven World Cup titles have been won by three nations – Italy, Germany, and England. But four other European countries have reached the World Cup final – Hungary, Sweden, the Netherlands, and Czechoslovakia – and there are a dozen others capable of beating the best.

△*Jean-Pierre Papin (in blue) scores for France against Belgium in the match for third place in the 1986 World Cup in Mexico. France won 4-2, but it was little consolation for losing to Germany in the semifinals for the second successive World Cup.*

The South Americans have a reputation for playing skillful, entertaining soccer. The game is an important part of life on the continent and is enjoyed by people from all walks of life.

Like Europe, South America has won seven World Cup titles, earned by three countries – Brazil, Argentina, and Uruguay. Of the other South American nations, Peruvian teams have recorded some fine wins over leading nations, and Chile reached the World Cup semifinals in 1962, when they hosted the finals tournament.

▽ *Peru's Teofilo Cubillas (left) attacks the Polish defense in the 1978 World Cup. Few players have scored more than his 10 goals in two World Cups, and he helped Peru reach the last eight in both 1970 and 1978.*

Brazil

The "Samba Kings" from South America are the great entertainers of soccer, and their three World Cup victories have all been won with a touch of magic.

In Brazil, soccer is an expression of the people. Like anyone else, Brazilians want their team to win, but they want them to do it with style.

Brazil won the World Cup in 1958, 1962, and 1970 – the first country to chalk up a hat trick of victories. And on each occasion they showed the world how soccer should be played.

Most Brazilian soccer players adopt playing names, and the great ones are remembered wherever soccer is played – Garrincha, Didi, Vavá, Jairzinho, Rivelino, Gerson, Socrates, Zico, and, above all, Pelé.

△ *Pelé (left) raises his arms to celebrate a Brazilian goal in the 1958 World Cup final against the host country Sweden. The young Pelé scored twice in this game.*

When the World Cup finals were held in their own country in 1950, the Brazilians were desperately disappointed to lose to Uruguay in the deciding match. A world record 200,000 people filled the great Maracaña Stadium that day.

Brazil tasted victory at last in 1958, in Sweden, inspired by the 17-year-old Pelé. Apart from his two goals in the final, he hit a hat trick against France in the semifinals. And although injury kept him out of the 1962 final and cut short his 1966 World Cup, he was back in 1970 to lead the team to further glory.

Brazil – facts and feats

✔ Brazil is the only country to have competed in the final stages of every World Cup.
✔ Brazil used only 12 men (instead of at least 16) in 1962, when they retained the trophy they had won four years earlier. Pelé was hurt in the second of the six games and Amarildo substituted.
✔ Brazil kept the original cup, the Jules Rimet Trophy, when the team won it in 1970 for the third time.

◁ *Pelé rejoices again, this time after scoring against Italy in the 1970 final.*

Argentina

Controversy seems to follow Argentina wherever the team goes. But they have won two World Cups in great style, and have played some dazzling soccer.

After finishing runner-up in the 1930 World Cup, Argentina was overshadowed by their rivals, first Uruguay and then Brazil, for nearly 50 years. Argentina failed to progress further than the first round of the finals until 1966.

The team finally won the Cup in 1978 as host country, but not without much controversy. In the first round, opposing team Hungary had two men ejected. In the second round, Argentina needed to beat Peru 4-0 to oust Brazil and reach the final – Peru's Argentinian-born goalkeeper let in six! And in the final, players kept the Dutch team waiting for 10 minutes while they protested against a plaster cast on an opponent's wrist.

Argentina – facts and feats

✔ Argentina's speedy center-forward Guillermo Stabile scored eight goals in the first World Cup, a record that was not beaten for 20 years.

✔ The 1986 final, in which Argentina beat Germany 3-2, was seen live on TV by 580 million people in 160 countries.

✔ The first player to be ejected in a World Cup final was Pedro Monzon of Argentina, in 1990, soon to be followed by teammate Gustavo Dezotti.

Argentina's performance in the 1978 final won the team many friends. They played some wonderful soccer, beating the Netherlands 3-1 in overtime.

Goalkeeper Ubaldo Fillol was outstanding, as was captain and sweeper Daniel Passarella. Osvaldo Ardiles was the perfect midfield link, and player of the tournament Mario Kempes scored twice in the final.

The 1986 team owed its success largely to the genius of Maradona.

▷ **Diego Maradona proudly poses with the World Cup after leading Argentina to victory in Mexico in 1986. He was the outstanding player of that World Cup, and made the pass for Jorge Burruchaga to score a spectacular winning goal in the final.**

The 1990 team was not nearly as good, but Maradona, despite suffering from an injury, still managed to get them to the final.

◁ **Osvaldo Ardiles (opposite page) weaves his way through the Dutch defense in the 1978 World Cup final. He was one of the stars of Argentina's triumph, with his tackling, pinpoint passing, and elusive running in midfield. He later became an extremely popular figure in England with Tottenham – for his sportsmanship as well as his soccer.**

Germany

Germany's fine record in the World Cup has been built on good organization, but this team has also played some wonderful soccer.

◁ *Center-forward Max Morlock (white shirt, on the ground) beats Hungarian goalkeeper Gyula Grosics to start Germany's recovery from 2-0 down in the 1954 final.*

▽ *Skipper Lothar Matthäus attacks the Argentinian defense in the 1990 World Cup final. He was the driving midfield force in a solid, but not exceptional, team.*

German teams have been the most consistent European competitors in the World Cup, and they have enjoyed more success even than the Brazilians. They did not enter the first tournament, and they were not invited in 1950, after World War II. But they have qualified for every other World Cup, have won it three times, and have been runners-up three times.

In 1954, Germany beat the strong favorite Hungary in the final to win the World Cup for the first time. They hosted the 1974 tournament and beat a talented Dutch team 2-1 in the final.

▷ *Midfielder Thomas Hässler emerged as a bright hope in Germany's bid for the 1994 World Cup with some fine performances in the 1992 European Championships. He's seen here in Germany's game against Scotland, which Germany won 2-0.*

In both 1954 and 1970, Germany came from behind to win the final. The team showed the same grit in 1966, tying with England in the last minute before losing in overtime. In 1970, they recovered from 2-0 down in the quarter-finals to beat England 3-2. And in the 1986 final, they were down by two and being handled easily by Argentina with only 17 minutes left when they came back and tied the game. They finally lost 3-2.

In 1990, Germany gained revenge by beating Argentina 1-0 in the final, scoring a disputed penalty with five minutes to go. But unfortunately it was a poor, bad-tempered match, with two Argentinian players ejected.

Germany – facts and feats

✔ *Franz Beckenbauer led Germany to World Cup victory as captain in 1974 and again as manager in 1990.*
✔ *Germany has reached the final of the World Cup six times, more than any other country.*
✔ *In the first stage of the 1954 finals, Germany lost 8-3 to Hungary. Having defeated Turkey 4-1, they beat them again in a play-off 7-2 and went on to beat Hungary 3-2 in the final.*

Note: From 1945 to 1990, Germany was split into East and West. East Germany qualified for the finals tournament only once (1974), when the team reached the second stage. They are now one country again, and for the purposes of this book, West Germany has been called Germany.

Italy

The Italians play soccer with passion. They are the Brazilians of Europe, but have never scaled the heights of Brazilian soccer at its best.

◁ *Manager Pozzo, holding the Jules Rimet Trophy, celebrates with his team after their 4-2 victory over Hungary in 1938.*

▽ *Italy's Paolo Rossi (blue shirt) and Brazil's Cerezo in the 1982 World Cup. Rossi's hat trick gave Italy a surprising 3-2 victory over the favorites on their way to a third Italian World Cup triumph.*

*I*taly became the second team to win three World Cups when they beat Germany 3-1 in the 1982 final. Their earlier successes had come in the 1930s.

The man who is remembered for leading Italy to victory in 1934 and 1938 is manager Vittorio Pozzo. He blended power with skill to produce his world-beating teams.

After World War II, Italy struggled for international success despite its many skilled players. The Italians failed to get past the first round of the World Cup until 1970, when they lost in the final to the brilliant Brazilians.

▷ *Gianluigi Lentini on the ball for Italian club AC Milan, who paid Torino a world record $26 million for him in 1992. Lentini and other talented Italians make their country one of the leading challengers for success again in the 1994 World Cup.*

Italy has acquired a reputation as one of the strongest soccer-playing countries in Europe, with perhaps the meanest defense in the world. But Italy rarely fulfills its promise and has suffered some shocking results in the World Cup.

In 1966 the Italians were eliminated by the unknown North Koreans. Even when they reached the final in 1970, they had scraped through the first round with only one goal in three games.

After another shaky start in 1982, Paolo Rossi hit goal-scoring form and Italy went on to beat Germany 3-1 in the final. In 1990, as hosts, Italy was the favorite, but the team was knocked out of the semifinals in a shoot-out with Argentina.

Italy – facts and feats

✔ Italy's Guiseppe Meazza and Giovanni Ferrari are the only Europeans to win two World Cup winners' medals, in 1934 and 1938.
✔ Two goalkeepers have captained successful World Cup teams – both Italian – Giampiero Combi in 1934 and Dino Zoff in 1982. Zoff, at 40 years, was the oldest player ever to win a World Cup winner's medal.
✔ Another Italian goalie to earn World Cup fame was Walter Zenga, who did not concede a goal for a record 8 hours and 37 minutes (5 matches and part of the 6th) in the 1990 tournament.
✔ Italy's first match in a World Cup finals tournament was a 7-1 win over the United States in Rome in 1934. Italy went on to win the Cup.

England

Soccer fans still argue about England's third goal in the 1966 World Cup – did the ball cross the line after Hurst's shot bounced down off the crossbar?

Britain, the home of soccer, had no teams in the World Cup until 1950. Before then the British soccer authorities had been in dispute with FIFA, the world's governing body.

England soon found that the rest of the world had caught up with them, and in their first four World Cups managed to reach only the quarterfinals twice. But they were hosts for the 1966 World Cup, and after a shaky start they went from strength to strength. Led by Bobby Moore, the team beat Argentina in the last eight, then Portugal, and, in the final, Germany by 4-2.

▽ *England's controversial third goal in the 1966 World Cup final. Geoff Hurst (right of picture) has just hooked the ball onto the crossbar. England claimed a goal, and the linesman confirmed to the referee that the ball had bounced down over the line. Film and video replays have never quite settled the argument.*

▷ **England's Paul Gascoigne takes the ball between two German defenders in the 1990 World Cup semifinal that Germany won in a shoot-out. Gascoigne was a star of the 1990 tournament, and England's hopes for 1994 rest largely on his shoulders.**

*E*ngland was unlucky in the defense of its title in the 1970 World Cup in Mexico. The team reached the last eight despite losing 1-0 to Brazil in a thrilling group match. Goalkeeper Gordon Banks was sick and could not play in the game against Germany. But England led 2-0 before going down 3-2 after overtime.

In 1982, England was unbeaten, but two tie games in the second stage was not good enough to take the team any further. In 1986, the team lost to Argentina in the quarterfinals. And in 1990 they lost to Germany in a shoot-out in the semifinals.

England – facts and feats

✔ *The quickest goal ever in a World Cup finals tournament was scored by England captain Bryan Robson against France in the first group game of the 1982 tournament – in just 27 seconds.*
✔ *England lost the World Cup before they won it in 1966. It was stolen while on display before the tournament, but was found just in time under a hedge by a dog named Pickles.*
✔ *Manager Alf Ramsey, a former international fullback, was knighted shortly after he guided England to its 1966 World Cup victory.*
✔ *Brothers Bobby and Jack Charlton played on England's winning 1966 team.*

Netherlands

The Netherlands emerged in the 1970s as the team to take over from Brazil as soccer's great entertainers – but they couldn't win the World Cup.

◁ *Marco van Basten (orange shirt) in action for the Netherlands in the 1990 World Cup. A striker with all the gifts, he was voted World Footballer of the Year in 1992 for the second time and European Footballer of the Year for the third time.*

Most neutral soccer fans were rooting for the Netherlands when they reached the finals of the 1974 and 1978 World Cups. Before then, they had played only two matches in finals tournaments, both first-round defeats, in 1934 and 1938.

The Netherlands first became a force in world soccer in the early 1970s. Success started with its top clubs Feyenoord and Ajax Amsterdam. It continued with the national team, inspired by the sparkling Johan Cruyff and driven by the midfield dynamo Johan Neeskens. The team played what became known as "total soccer." It was a thrilling, spirited style in which all of the players (except the goalkeeper) could perform in any position, and the accent was on offense.

▷ *Dennis Bergkamp (number 7, opposite page) bursts between two Danish players in the 1992 European Championships. His performances as an offensive midfielder in this tournament were world class.*

In the 1974 World Cup, the Netherlands beat the might of South America – Uruguay, Argentina, and Brazil – on the way to the final. But although they outplayed host country Germany for much of the final, they lost 2-1.

It was a similar story in 1978. The team emerged top of a second-round group that included Italy and Germany to reach the final. But they lost again to the host country, Argentina.

With stars such as Ruud Gullit, Marco van Basten, and Frank Rijkaard, the Netherlands won the 1988 European Championships, but disappointed in the 1990 World Cup.

Netherlands – facts and feats

✔ When Johan Neeskens scored from a penalty after 78 seconds of the 1974 World Cup final against Germany, no opponent had touched the ball.

✔ Dutch striker Robbie Rensenbrink scored the 1,000th goal in World Cup final tournaments – a penalty against Scotland in 1978.

✔ Dutch midfielder Arie Haan had one of the hardest shots ever seen. In the 1978 World Cup, he scored from 32 yards against Germany and then hit home a 38-yard free kick past Italian goalie Dino Zoff.

✔ Dirk Nanninga was ejected in a group match against Germany in the 1978 World Cup, but went on as a substitute in the final and scored the Dutch goal.

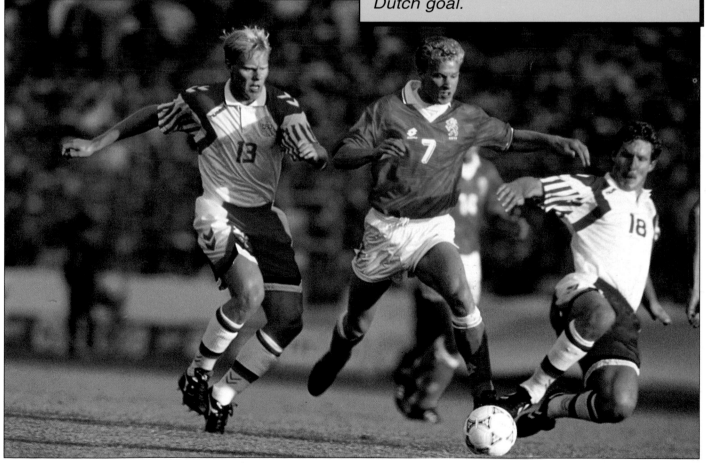

Ireland

Nobody can ever afford to treat the Irish lightly. Since Jack Charlton became manager in February 1986, their blend of skill and spirit has achieved considerable success.

For a small country of fewer than four million people, the Republic's recent results have been remarkable. Charlton is undoubtedly helped by the strange FIFA rules that allow players to qualify as Irish by reason of family connections. (These rules apply to players for any nation.) Ireland's John Aldridge, Andy Townsend, and Ray Houghton would not be out of place in other more distinguished national teams.

The Republic first qualified for the World Cup finals in 1990, astounding everybody by reaching the quarterfinals and losing unluckily to Italy, by the only goal of the match.

▽ **Andy Townsend (left) in action for the Republic of Ireland against Romania in the 1990 World Cup.**

Ireland – facts and feats

✔ The Republic tied all three first-round matches in the 1990 World Cup: 1-1 with England, 0-0 with Egypt, and 1-1 with Holland. In the second round they beat Romania 5-4 in a shoot-out, thanks to a dramatic save by goalie Pat Bonner.

✔ In 1950 the Republic became the first team from outside the United Kingdom to beat England in England. They won 2-0 at Everton.

✔ Con Martin played for Leeds, Aston Villa, the Republic, and Northern Ireland in the 1940s and 1950s, scoring only two League goals in a 10-year career. But he scored four in 34 internationals, all in the 1949–50 season. Usually a fullback or halfback, he also played goalie.

Denmark

Many leading players leave Denmark to earn greater fame and fortune on teams from other countries, but fortunately the supply of talent shows few signs of drying up.

◁ *Goalkeeper Peter Schmeichel in action for Denmark in the European Championships. Like many of his teammates, he plays his club soccer outside Denmark, in his case for Manchester United in England.*

Denmark reached the World Cup finals tournament for the first time in 1986. They played some of the best soccer of the competition, coming in first of their first-round group. The teams they beat were Scotland (1-0), Uruguay (6-1), and Germany (2-0). Then, disappointingly, they were knocked out 5-1 by Spain in the last 16.

Denmark has done well in the European Football Championships, which have been held every four years since 1960. The team reached the semifinals in 1964 and 1984, and the last eight in 1988. They then surprised everyone by winning the 1992 tournament after coming into it at the last moment to replace another country.

Denmark – facts and feats

✔ *Professional soccer was not introduced in Denmark until 1978, but the country had built a proud amateur record before then, winning the Olympic soccer tournament once and being runners-up three times.*

✔ *Group E of the 1978 World Cup finals was called "The Group of Death" by Uruguyan coach Omar Borras when he found that his country had been drawn with Denmark, Germany, and Scotland.*

✔ *Preben Elkjaer, who scored a hat trick against Uruguay in 1986, was only one of the many Danes to have played in other countries. Karl Praest, Allan Simonsen, Michael and Brian Laudrup, Jesper Olsen, and Jan Molby are among the others.*

✔ *Elkjaer was the top scorer, with eight goals, in the qualifying tournament for the 1986 World Cup.*

Sweden

Followers of soccer in Sweden still long for a repeat of their team's success in 1958, when their country hosted the World Cup finals tournament.

△ **Nils Liedholm scores a penalty against Mexico in the 1958 World Cup. Like four of his teammates, he was with an Italian club at the time.**

*F*ew of the smaller soccer-playing nations can match Sweden's record. In addition to hosting the 1958 World Cup tournament, when Sweden reached the final, the team has qualified for seven other tournaments, finishing third once and fourth once. Arguably their greatest team came together for the 1958 event, and if they had met any team other than Brazil in the final they might well have won.

The coach of the 1958 team was faced with a problem because the best Swedish soccer players were playing for Italian clubs. Fortunately a Swedish FA rule forbidding foreign-based players from appearing for their own country was altered just in time.

Sweden – facts and feats

✔ Sven Jonasson of Sweden scored the 100th goal in World Cup finals during the 1934 tournament, and fellow countryman Gustav Wetterstroem scored the 200th four years later.

✔ Hans Jeppson, who scored two goals for Sweden when they beat Italy 3-2 in the 1950 World Cup, later played for the English club Charlton Athletic as an amateur.

✔ George Raynor, who did so much as Sweden's coach in the 1950s, was wisely given the job although he was only assistant trainer of Aldershot at the time the offer was made.

✔ Sweden won the Olympic Games soccer tournament in 1948 and has placed third twice.

Norway

England, France, Italy, and Argentina have all lost in Oslo during recent years, indicating that Norway may even yet be making up for lost time.

The history of Norwegian involvement in the World Cup finals takes little telling: it consists of one match only. But what a match – a thrilling 2-1 defeat by world champions Italy in 1938, when the competition was played on a straight single-elimination basis. Italy went on to win the Cup.

Norway had lost to Italy by the same score in the 1936 Olympic games semifinal, after remarkably beating host nation Germany 2-0. The German Fuehrer, Adolf Hitler, stormed from the stadium at the end. Six of the players from 1936 remained in 1938, including wing Arne Brustad, who played for the Rest of Europe against England a few weeks later.

Norway – facts and feats

✔ Jurgen Juve, who captained Norway to third place in the 1936 Olympics, is still his country's top international scorer, with 33 goals.
✔ Thorbjorn Svensson played 104 times for Norway and is thought to be the first man from any country to top 100 in full internationals.

◁ **Norway celebrates tying the score at 1-1 against England in a World Cup qualifying match at Wembley in October 1992. Norway went on to defeat England 2-0 in the return match in Oslo.**

U.S. – host for 1994

Host for the 1994 finals tournament, the United States has never been a strong soccer-playing country, although the game is becoming increasingly popular in schools.

The United States reached the World Cup finals tournament for only the fourth time in 1990, although the team brought off one of the greatest upsets in World Cup history when they beat England 1-0 in the 1950 competition, staged in Brazil.

Soccer has to take a back seat in the United States to the American code of football. Professional leagues have rarely lasted for long because they have depended on foreign stars, and the best U.S. players are now being snapped up by European clubs. But soccer is becoming more and more popular at school, with girls as well as boys playing the game to a high standard.

△ *Action from the Italy-U.S. game in 1990 (U.S. playing in white). The United States qualified for the first time since 1950. They lost all three games, but did surprisingly well to hold host country Italy to 1-0.*

▷ *Larry Gaetjens of the United States (left of picture) beats England goalkeeper Bert Williams to score the only goal of the game in the 1950 World Cup tournament. England had been joint favorites with Brazil to win the World Cup, yet were beaten by a team of part-timers from the U.S.*

Women lead the way

The first Women's World Cup was held in China in 1991. The U.S. (seen here in white, playing Japan) won the Cup, with victories in all six of their matches. The U.S. scored most goals (25, against 5) and provided the player of the tournament in Michelle Akers-Stahl, the top scorer with 10 goals.

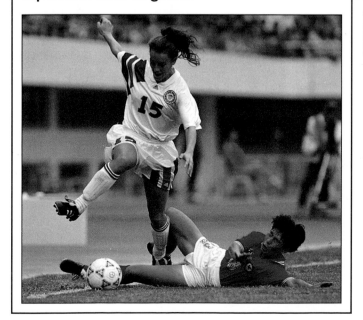

United States – facts and feats

✔ *The U.S. is among the few countries to have entered every World Cup, although the team withdrew in 1938 before playing a match.*

✔ *One of only 13 countries to enter the first World Cup, in 1930, the United States reached the semifinals. The team beat both Belgium and Paraguay 3-0 before losing 6-1 to Argentina.*

✔ *The U.S. team's biggest defeat in the finals tournament came in 1934, when they lost 7-1 to Italy in the first round.*

Rising powers

Countries from Europe and South America have dominated the World Cup for 60 years, but are now seriously being challenged, especially by teams from Africa.

When the unknown soccer players from North Korea surprised the world with their performances in the 1966 World Cup, followers of the game thought a new soccer power had been born. But the Koreans never repeated those successes, and after that there was just an occasional upset from the continents of Asia and Africa. Then, in the 1980s, things began to change.

△ *North Korea (dark shirts) beat Italy 1-0 in the 1966 World Cup after tying with Chile and qualified for the quarterfinals. They sensationally led Portugal 3-0, but finally lost 5-3.*

Cameroon and Algeria from Africa gave the first warnings of a new, emerging soccer power in 1982. Cameroon was unbeaten in its first-round group, tying all three matches and conceding just one goal, to Italy. Italy also tied its games, but went through to the next stage because the team scored more goals. Algeria's performance was even better. They beat Germany and Chile, but still failed on goal difference.

In 1986, an African team finished first in its group. Morocco tied with Poland and England, and beat Portugal 3-1. The Moroccans were beaten only 1-0 by Germany in the second round.

It was Cameroon again in 1990 who made its presence felt. Cameroon beat World Cup holders Argentina and then Romania to win its group, and reached the quarterfinals by beating Colombia, but lost to England 3-2.

Egypt also showed how African soccer had improved, tying in 1990 with the Netherlands and the Republic of Ireland before losing 1-0 to England.

▽ *Cameroon (green and red) gave England a scare in the 1990 quarterfinals before losing 3-2.*

Facts and figures

World Cup finals tournaments

Most wins	3	Brazil, Italy, Germany
Most appearances	14	Brazil
Most World Cup finals	6	Germany
Highest score in final	5	Brazil (1958)
Highest score in match	10	Hungary (1982, beat El Salvador 10-1)
Highest score in qualifying match	13	New Zealand (1981, beat Fiji 13-0)
Highest aggregate score	12	(1954, Austria 7 Switzerland 5)
Most individual goals	14	Gerd Müller, Germany (10 in 1970, 4 in 1974)
Most in one tournament	13	Just Fontaine, France (1958)
Most in World Cup final	3	Geoff Hurst, England (1966)
Most games played	21	Uwe Seeler (Germany 1958-70)
		Wladyslaw Zmuda (Poland 1974-86)
Youngest player		Norman Whiteside (Northern Ireland, 1982)
		He was 17 years and 42 days old.
Biggest attendance	200,000	(Brazil v. Uruguay, Maracaña Stadium, 1950)

World Cup finals

Year	Host	Result
1930	Uruguay	Uruguay 4 Argentina 2
1934	Italy	*Italy 2 Czechoslovakia 1
1938	France	Italy 4 Hungary 2
1950	Brazil	†Uruguay 2 Brazil 1
1954	Switzerland	Germany 3 Hungary 2
1958	Sweden	Brazil 5 Sweden 2
1962	Chile	Brazil 3 Czechoslovakia 1
1966	England	*England 4 Germany 2
1970	Mexico	Brazil 4 Italy 1
1974	Germany	Germany 2 Netherlands 1
1978	Argentina	*Argentina 3 Netherlands 1
1982	Spain	Italy 3 Germany 1
1986	Mexico	Argentina 3 Germany 2
1990	Italy	Germany 1 Argentina 0

*In overtime.   †Deciding match of final pool.

Leading scorers in finals

Year	No.	Player (Country)
1930	8	Guillermo Stabile (Argentina)
1934	4	Edmund Conen (Germany)
		Angelo Schiavio (Italy)
		Oldrich Nejedly (Czechoslovakia)
1938	8	Leonidas da Silva (Brazil)
1950	9	Ademir (Brazil)
1954	11	Sandor Kocsis (Hungary)
1958	13	Just Fontaine (France)
1962	5	Drazen Jerkovic (Yugoslavia)
1966	9	Eusebio (Portugal)
1970	10	Gerd Müller (Germany)
1974	7	Grzegorz Lato (Poland)
1978	6	Mario Kempes (Argentina)
1982	6	Paolo Rossi (Italy)
1986	6	Gary Lineker (England)
1990	6	Salvatore Schillaci (Italy)

Four goals in a game

Nine players have scored four goals in a game in a finals tournament. Two of them did so in the same game! This was a first-round match at Strasbourg, France, in 1938, between Brazil and Poland. After 90 minutes, the score was 4-4, and Brazil won 6-5 after overtime. Leonidas scored four for Brazil, and Willimowski four for Poland.

The full list of individual four-goal scorers is:

Gustav Wetterstroem (Sweden v. Cuba 1938)

Leonidas da Silva (Brazil v. Poland 1938)

Ernest Willimowski (Poland v. Brazil 1938)

Ademir (Brazil v. Sweden 1950)

Juan Schiaffino (Uruguay v. Bolivia 1950)

Sandor Kocsis (Hungary v. Germany 1954)

Just Fontaine (France v. Germany 1958)

Eusebio (Portugal v. North Korea 1966)

Emilio Butragueño (Spain v. Denmark 1986)

◁ **Sandor Kocsis, who scored four goals for Hungary against Germany in a 1954 World Cup first-round match.**

War games

The qualifying games between El Salvador and Honduras in 1969 caused a war between the two Central American countries. There had been conflict between the countries, but things boiled over when they clashed on the soccer field, sparking a full-scale war that lasted two weeks. Hostilities eventually died down, and El Salvador won a play-off. They went on to qualify for the World Cup, but lost all three of their matches in the finals in Mexico without scoring a goal.

Goals per game

The number of games played in finals tournaments has increased from fewer than 20 in the 1930s to 52 in modern times. However, goal-scoring has gone down. The record is an average of 5.38 per game, set in 1954, when 140 goals were scored in 26 games. Since then the only tournament to produce more goals has been 1982, when 146 goals were scored in 52 games, an average of 2.81. The lowest average was 2.21 in 1990, only 115 goals in 52 games.

Mascots

There have been official mascots, used to publicize the World Cup tournament, since 1966. "World Cup Willie" (a lion) was the mascot in England in 1966. Other mascots have included "Tip and Tap" (children) in Germany (1974), "Gauchito" (cowboy) in Argentina (1978) and "Naranjito" (an orange) in Spain (1982). The mascot for the 1994 World Cup in the U.S. is a "lucky dog, symbolizing youth, vitality, and soccer fever" and is called "Striker."

Women's World Cup

The finals of the first Women's World Cup were played in China in 1991. After competitions in various continents, 12 teams qualified for the finals tournament. They played in three groups of four countries, and eight won through to the next round, the quarterfinals.

Europe provided five of the last eight, and when Sweden beat the hosts China 1-0, there were three European teams left in the semifinals together with the U.S. Norway beat Sweden 4-1 and the U.S. beat Germany 5-2. In the final, the U.S. defeated Norway 2-1 before an audience of 65,000 in Canton.

Glossary

Cap
In many countries, players are awarded a cap when they play for their country. If a player has won 100 caps, it means he or she has made 100 appearances for his or her country in full internationals.

Caution
An official warning, or "booking," by the referee, who takes the offending player's name and displays a yellow card. A player is ejected for a second caution in a match. In the World Cup and some other big competitions, a player cannot play in the next match if he or she receives two cautions in the competition.

Dismissal
A punishment for certain offenses in which a player is ejected from the field for the remainder of the game by the referee, who indicates the decision by displaying a red card.

Dissent
Showing disagreement with a referee's decision. Dissent is an offense.

FIFA
The Fédération Internationale de Football Association, the world governing body of soccer.

Foul
An intentional offense on an opponent, punishable by a free kick or, if committed in the penalty area, by a penalty kick. If a player fouls an opponent who, in the opinion of the referee, has an obvious goal-scoring opportunity, it is regarded as "serious foul play" and the offender is ejected. Such an offense is often referred to as a "professional foul." An illegal handball is, in the same way, punishable by ejection.

Goal difference
A method used to determine positions in a group or league when two or more teams have the same number of points. To work out the goal difference, you subtract the goals conceded from the goals scored.

Group
A number of teams in a competition that play each other to qualify for the next stage.

Hat trick
The scoring of three goals by a player in a game.

Host country
The country that stages the finals tournament of the World Cup.

Marking
Staying close to an opponent to try to prevent him or her from receiving or using the ball. "Man-for-man marking" is a method in which each defender is responsible for marking a particular opponent, wherever he or she moves.

Midfield general

A player who controls the offense from midfield, also called a "play-maker" or "schemer." Not all teams have a midfield general, because the role calls for outstanding ball control, passing ability, vision, and tactical awareness.

Overtime

A period or periods played when scores are tied after 90 minutes.

Qualifying competition

The games played to decide which countries go to the World Cup finals tournament.

Shoot-out

A method for deciding a game when the scores are still tied after overtime.

Single-elimination stage

The stage of a tournament when the winners of each match go on to the next round and the losers are eliminated.

Sponsor

A company that pays money to a player, team, or competition in return for advertising.

Squad

The players that a team is chosen from. Major competitions have a maximum number of players in a squad, from which 11 players take the field and five (more in some tournaments) are nominated as substitutes. In most competitions, only two substitutes may be used.

Sweeper

A player who operates behind the defense, given a free hand to stop danger and support fellow defenders, without marking duties. An "attacking sweeper" plays in front of the defense.

Target man

A striker whose chief job is to control passes upfield from defense and midfield, holding the ball until his or her teammates arrive to help.

Zone defense

A method of play in which the defenders are each responsible for a particular part, or zone, of the field, marking or tackling any opposing player who comes into that zone.

Books to read

Arnold, Catherine. *Soccer: From Neighborhood Play to the World Cup*. First Books. Franklin Watts: New York, 1991.

Dewazien, Karl. *Fundamental Soccer Practice*. Clovis, CA: Fun Soccer Enterprises, 1987.

Dolan, Edward F. *Starting Soccer: A Handbook for Boys and Girls*. New York: HarperCollins Children's Books, 1976.

Goodman, Michael. *The World Cup*. Mankato, MN: Creative Education, 1990.

Sakurai, Jennifer. *Rules of the Game: Soccer*. Los Angeles: Price Stern Sloane, 1990.

Yannis, Alex. *Soccer Basics*. New York: Prentice Hall, 1982.

Index